RELIGIONS AROUND THE WORLD

Buddhism

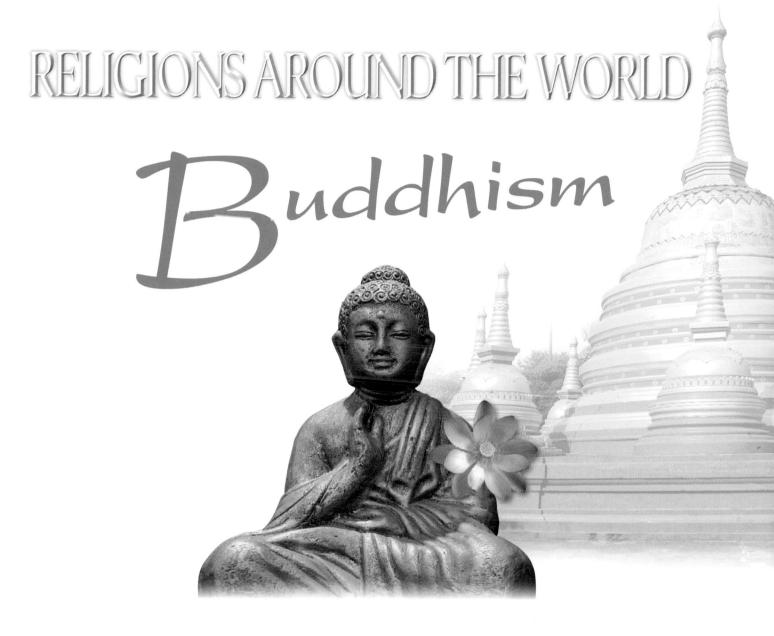

Katy Gerner

 **Marshall Cavendish**
Benchmark

New York

This edition first published in 2009 in the United States of America by Marshall Cavendish Benchmark.

Marshall Cavendish Benchmark
99 White Plains Road
Tarrytown, NY 10591
www.marshallcavendish.us

First published in 2008 by
MACMILLAN EDUCATION AUSTRALIA PTY LTD
15–19 Claremont Street, South Yarra 3141

Visit our website at www.macmillan.com.au or go directly to www.macmillanlibrary.com.au

Associated companies and representatives throughout the world.

Copyright © Katy Gerner 2008

Library of Congress Cataloging-in-Publication Data

Gerner, Katy.
    Buddhism / by Katy Gerner.
        p. cm. — (Religions around the world)
    Includes index.
    ISBN 978-0-7614-3164-0
    1. Buddhism—Juvenile literature. I. Title.
    BQ4032.G47 2008
294.3—dc22
                            2008002859

Edited by Erin Richards
Text and cover design by Cristina Neri, Canary Graphic Design
Photo research by Legend Images
Illustration on p. 14 by Andy Craig and Nives Porcellato
Map courtesy of Geo Atlas; modified by Raul Diche

Printed in the United States

Acknowledgments

The author would like to thank Lama Kalzang Norbu for his suggestions, his wisdom and his time spent reviewing this book.

The author and the publisher are grateful to the following for permission to reproduce copyright material:

Front cover photograph (main): Tibetan nuns at a monastery in Nepal © Paula Bronstein/Getty Images. Other images: gold statue of Buddha © chad breece/iStockphoto; Phra Siratana Chedi, Grand Palace, Bangkok, Thailand © Pavel Pospisil/iStockphoto; book background © Felix Möckel/iStockphoto; lotus flower © Daniel Baumgartner/iStockphoto; Wheel of Samsara © Chrystal Henkaline/ iStockphoto; Golden pagoda, Myanmar © Alan Tobey/iStockphoto; Statue of Buddha in Thailand © John Hemmings/Shutterstock.

Photos courtesy of: © Elena Pokrovskaya/123RF, 5 (bottom); © Micha Rosenwirth/123RF, 11 (bottom left); © Philip Baird/www. anthroarcheart.org, 13 (right); Buddhist Compassion Relief Tzu Chi Foundation, 18 (left); © Steve Raymer/CORBIS, 26 (top); © Kapoor Baldev/Sygma/CORBIS, 27; The DW Stock Picture Library, 28; © chad breece/iStockphoto, 1 (left), 5 (top); © Edward Hardam/iStockphoto, 31 (top); © Chrystal Henkaline/iStockphoto, 5 (center); © Aman Khan/iStockphoto, 4 (bottom centre left); © Vasko Miokovic/iStockphoto, 4 (center); © Owusu-Ansah/iStockphoto, 4 (bottom centre right); © José Carlos Pires Pereira/ iStockphoto, 8; © Richard Stamper/iStockphoto, 4 (bottom right), 30 (top right); © Bob Thomas/iStockphoto, 4 (bottom left); Khem Sovannara/AFP/Getty Images, 21 (top); Getty Images/Simon Cook/The Bridgeman Art Library, 29; Paula Bronstein/Getty Images, 9 (bottom); Robert Nickelsberg/Time Life Pictures/Getty Images, 11 (bottom right); NASA Goddard Space Flight Center, 4 (center behind); Pelusey Photography, 24; © ArkReligion.com/Alamy/Photolibrary, 23; © EmmePi Travel/Alamy/Photolibrary, 6; © LOOK Die Bildagentur der Fotografen GmbH/Alamy/Photolibrary, 10 (top); © John Hemmings/Shutterstock, 3 (center), 12 (left); © Bartlomiej K. Kwieciszewski/Shutterstock, 7 (bottom); © Petr Meshkov/Shutterstock, 19 (bottom right); © Lily Rosen – Zohar/ Shutterstock, 22 (bottom); © Gina Smith/Shutterstock, 16 (top); © Juha Sompinmäki/Shutterstock, 20 (bottom right); © Gordon Swanson/Shutterstock, 4 (bottom); © Bruce Yeung/Shutterstock, 25 (bottom); © Huang Yuetao/Shutterstock, 20 (bottom left); U.S. Navy photo by Photographer's Mate 3rd Class Ian W. Anderson, 17 (bottom); Ralf-André Lettau, Wikimedia Commons, 15.

Photos used in book design: book background © Felix Möckel/iStockphoto, 11, 19; Buddhist temple by Ralf-André Lettau, Wikimedia Commons, 1; Wheel of Samsara © Chrystal Henkaline/iStockphoto, 17; lotus flower © Daniel Baumgartner/iStockphoto, 1, 3, 16; parchment background © Andrey Zyk/iStockphoto, 12, 13, 18, 19; Phra Siratana Chedi, Grand Palace, Bangkok, Thailand © Pavel Pospisil/iStockphoto, 3, 7, 9, 10, 14, 19, 20, 22, 25, 26, 30, 31, 32.

For everybody at Meredith Street

135642

Contents

Glossary words

When a word is printed in **bold**, you can look up its meaning in the Glossary on page 31.

World Religions

Religion is a belief in a supernatural power that must be loved, worshipped, and obeyed. A world religion is a religion that is practiced throughout the world. The five core world religions are Christianity, Islam, Hinduism, Buddhism and Judaism.

People practicing a religion follow practices that they believe are pleasing to their god or gods. Followers read sacred **scriptures** and may worship either privately at home or in a place of worship. They often carry out special rituals, such as when a baby is born, a couple gets married, or someone dies. Religious people have beliefs about how they should behave in this life, and also about life after death.

Learning about world religions can help us to understand each other's differences. We learn about the different ways people try to lead good lives and make the world a better place.

World religions are practiced by many people of different cultures.

Buddhism

Buddhism is the search for enlightenment, or **nirvana**. This is a state of mind in which a person is freed from everyday demands, confusion, and emotional attachment to things. Buddhists try to achieve enlightenment by developing wisdom, morality, and concentration.

There are two main streams of Buddhism. These streams are Theravada Buddhism and Mahayana Buddhism. The main aim of Theravada Buddhists is to achieve enlightenment for themselves. Mahayana Buddhists also aim to achieve enlightenment, but vow to help others achieve it as well. Mahayana Buddhists also pray to end suffering for all. A sub-class of Mahayana Buddhism is Tibetan Buddhism.

Buddhists **take refuge** in the Three Jewels, or Triple Gems. They are:

* the Buddha, a former Indian prince called Siddhartha Gautama, who was born more than 2,500 years ago
* the dharma, the teachings of Buddha
* the sangha, the community of Buddhist monks and nuns.

The Wheel of Samsara is the universal symbol of Buddhism.

The places where Buddhist monks live and worship are called monasteries.

Religious Beliefs

Many Buddhists do not believe in a god. They do believe in **karma**, and some Buddhists also believe in **deities** and **bodhisattvas**.

Karma

Buddhists believe that a person's actions give them good or bad karma. A Buddhist who does not achieve enlightenment in their lifetime will be reborn into one of six **realms** on the Wheel of Samsara. The realm into which a person is reborn depends on his or her karma.

The Wheel of Samsara

The six realms on the Wheel of Samsara are:

- Devas, the realm of gods
- Asuras, the realm of demigods
- Manushya, the human realm
- Tiryak, the animal realm
- Pretas, the realm of hungry ghosts
- Niraya, the hell realm.

People with bad karma are reborn into Niraya. There they experience much suffering until all their bad karma is used up. Only then can they be reborn into a higher realm. Similarly, people with good karma may be reborn into Devas, where they experience much pleasure. However, once their good karma is used up, they too are reborn into another realm.

The best realm in which to be reborn is the human realm. Only humans have the opportunity to achieve enlightenment and end the cycle of rebirth.

A depiction of the Wheel of Samsara

Deities and Bodhisattvas

Some Buddhists, particularly those practicing Tibetan Buddhism, believe in deities and bodhisattvas. Deities are supernatural beings who provide rainfall, good crops, wealth, children, and protection from danger. Bodhisattvas are people who have achieved enlightenment, but have postponed nirvana to help others achieve enlightenment.

Some Buddhists believe that by praying to a deity they will receive the deity's blessings. Buddhists from Tibet, Mongolia, and Nepal are very fond of the deity Tara. Tara is very beautiful and helps Buddhists reach nirvana. Some Tibetan Buddhists believe that Tara is a bodhisattva rather than a deity.

Dalai Lamas

Tibetan Buddhists believe that the **dalai lama** is the **incarnation** of Avalokiteshvara, the bodhisattva of compassion and patron saint of Tibet. Dalai lamas form a long line of reincarnated spiritual leaders that goes back to 1391 CE. The first dalai lama was Gedun Drupa, who lived from 1391 CE to 1474 CE. He wrote at least eight books on Buddha's teachings and philosophy. The second dalai lama, Gedun Gyatso, was born in 1475 CE and became an **abbot** of two monasteries. Today's Dalai Lama is believed to be the fourteenth incarnation of Avalokiteshvara.

These statues in Thailand are of Buddhist deities.

Beliefs About Behavior

Buddhist beliefs about behavior include following the Noble Eightfold Path and the Five Precepts. These were both taught by Buddha.

Noble Eightfold Path

The Noble Eightfold Path was taught by Buddha as the way to end personal suffering and unhappiness.

The eight elements of the Noble Eightfold Path are:

1 Right View (see the world as it really is)

2 Right Intention (commit yourself to what is good and positive)

3 Right Speech (speak kindly, warmly, gently, truthfully, and with purpose)

4 Right Action (do not kill, hurt, lie, or steal)

5 Right Livelihood (avoid jobs that harm living creatures and the environment)

6 Right Effort (control dangerous desires)

7 Right Mindfulness (be aware of your thoughts and actions)

8 Right Concentration (achieve a state of inner calm through meditation).

Buddha taught that following the Noble Eightfold Path is the only way to become enlightened and reach nirvana.

Buddhists practise meditation to achieve Right Concentration.

Five Precepts

Buddha also taught the Five Precepts. These precepts are meant to guide people in their everyday life.

The Five Precepts are:

1 I must avoid hurting living things

2 I must not steal from other people

3 I must not be involved in sexual misconduct

4 I must not lie or gossip

5 I must not drink alcohol or use drugs and other substances that cloud my thinking and make me behave rashly.

Precepts for Monks and Nuns

There are hundreds of other precepts for Theravada-ordained monks and nuns to follow. Some precepts that **novice monks** and nuns must follow include:

❀ I will not eat after noon each day

❀ I will not dance, sing, or go to the theatre

❀ I will not wear expensive clothes, jewelry, or perfume

❀ I will not sleep on a comfortable bed

❀ I will not have money.

Novice nuns must eat only in the mornings.

Scriptures

The complete Tripitaka uses 130,000 woodblocks.

There are a number of scriptures in Buddhism. The best known is the Pali Canon, or Tripitaka.

Pali Canon

The Pali Canon is made up of three texts and was originally taught and memorized around 600 BCE. The scriptures were written on palm leaves that were stored in baskets. This may be how it got the name *Tripitaka*, meaning "three baskets." The three texts are:

- Vinaya Pitaka
- Sutta Pitaka
- Abhidhamma Pitaka.

Today the Pali Canon is printed using woodblock printing. The text is carved into wooden blocks and paper is rubbed over them.

Vinaya Pitaka

The Vinaya Pitaka explains the precepts for monks and nuns. It also gives explanations and stories of how Buddha came to choose the monks and nuns as leaders of their religion.

Sutta Pitaka

The Sutta Pitaka contains more than 10,000 sayings of Buddha and his followers. It teaches about inner peace, self-control, good behavior, and feelings. It also includes Buddha's account of his own experience of enlightenment.

Exercising control in walking,
Standing,
Sitting,
And lying down ...
A monk who lives strictly like this,
Not restlessly, but at peace,
Always mindful,
Becomes more aware of peace.

ITIVUTTAKA 110,
KHUDDAKA NIKAYA IV, SUTTA PITAKA

Buddhist monks spend time each day studying the scriptures.

Abhidhamma Pitaka

The Abhidhamma Pitaka consists of seven books, which contain information on science and philosophy. One of the books, the Kathavatthu, contains more than two hundred debates on questions about religious beliefs. Another, the Puggalapannatti, contains information on personality types.

Tibetan prayer wheels have scriptures carved into them.

Religious Leaders

Two religious leaders important to Buddhists are Buddha, the founder of Buddhism, and King Asoka, who helped spread Buddha's teachings to many countries.

Buddha   563–483 BCE

Buddha, which means "The Fully Awakened One," was the founder of Buddhism. He was once Prince Siddhartha Gautama and lived in luxury until he became curious about the outside world. On his outings he saw a sick man, an old man, a dead body, and, finally, a peaceful holy man. These sights showed Siddhartha that everything is **impermanent**. Eventually he too would get sick, grow old, and die. Upset by this, he left his palaces and family to seek the cause of and cure for suffering.

For seven years the prince studied under holy men in the forests, but did not find the answer. He decided to sit under a tree and meditate until he did. The answers he found are the Four Noble Truths:

1 Life includes suffering

2 Suffering results from craving things

3 To eliminate suffering, eliminate craving

4 The path to the end of suffering is the Noble Eightfold Path.

Buddha spent the rest of his life teaching what he had learned. When he died he was not reborn as he had achieved nirvana.

Statues of Buddha often show him in a sitting position.

King Asoka
272–236 BCE

King Asoka lived in India and ruled over the Mauryan Kingdom. This kingdom included most of India and Pakistan, and parts of Bangladesh. King Asoka was originally a warrior king, known for his cruelty. He had murdered many people, including his brothers.

Eventually, King Asoka could not cope with violence any more and became a Buddhist. He stopped fighting, made peace with weaker kingdoms, and built hospitals, monasteries, and a Buddhist university. He ordered that trees be preserved, wells be dug along roads for thirsty travelers, roads be mended, and sick animals be cared for. He made himself available to his citizens any time of the day.

King Asoka sent his **disciples** to preach and teach the dharma as far away as Syria, Egypt, and Macedonia. It was these actions that helped Buddhism become a world religion.

King Asoka turned his back on violence when he became a Buddhist.

Worship Practices

Important worship practices for Buddhists include meditating at a temple and going on **pilgrimages**.

Meditating at a Temple

Meditating at a temple helps Buddhists develop and improve their faith and learn the methods of practicing the Noble Eightfold Path. Buddhists do not have to visit a temple at a set time on a set day. When visiting a temple, they usually take their shoes off. They never point the soles of their feet toward a statue or picture of Buddha, or toward a monk. This would be considered very rude and disrespectful.

Inside a temple Buddhists will usually:

❀ perform three **prostrations** to the statue of Buddha

❀ sit cross-legged or kneel in silence in front of the statue of Buddha

❀ listen to monks chanting from the Pali Canon

❀ recite prayers with other followers

❀ present incense, flowers, and lit candles as offerings

❀ ask to take refuge in the Three Jewels before a monk. This involves kneeling in front of the shrine, putting their hands together in front of their chest, prostrating themselves, and then reciting the Refuge Prayer.

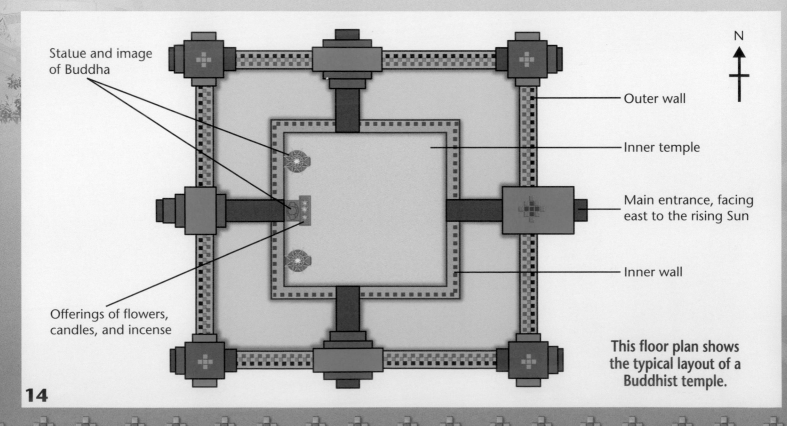

Statue and image of Buddha

Offerings of flowers, candles, and incense

N

Outer wall

Inner temple

Main entrance, facing east to the rising Sun

Inner wall

This floor plan shows the typical layout of a Buddhist temple.

Pilgrimages

A pilgrimage is a journey, often a long one, made to a sacred place. Buddhists are encouraged to go on pilgrimages to the places where important events in Buddha's life happened. Buddhists believe that these pilgrimages help them have a better life the next time they are reborn. They will have a better chance of breaking through the endless cycle of birth, life, death, and rebirth, and passing into nirvana. It also helps them to better understand Buddha's teachings and makes their faith stronger.

Buddhists go on pilgrimages to many places, including:

❁ Lumbini in Nepal, where Buddha was born
❁ Bodhgaya in Bihar, in India, where Buddha first achieved enlightenment
❁ Saranath in India, where Buddha began preaching sermons
❁ Kushinagar in Uttar Pradesh, in India, where Buddha passed on into nirvana.

The Lettau temple in Thailand is an important place of pilgrimage for Thai Buddhists.

Buddhists in South Korea celebrate Wesak with a procession of lanterns.

Festivals and Celebrations

Buddhist festivals and celebrations vary from country to country. They also depend on the type of Buddhism practiced.

Wesak

Wesak, also known as Buddha Day, is held in April or May. It is a celebration of the birth, enlightenment, and passing on of Buddha. Mahayana Buddhists celebrate the three events on three separate days. Others celebrate it on the day of the full moon in April or May.

It is important to be generous during Wesak. Buddhists give gifts and new robes to the monks and some exchange small gifts and cards. Children are told stories about Buddha's past lives and each story teaches the children a moral lesson.

In Sri Lanka, homes and temples are decorated with lanterns and candles. In Thailand, Buddhists walk around the vihara, or Buddhist shrine, three times for the Three Jewels – once for Buddha, once for dharma and once for sangha. Then Wesak ends with a candlelit procession.

O-bon

O-bon is celebrated in July or August in Japan. It is a time for remembering ancestors and welcoming their spirits home for their yearly visit.

O-bon is celebrated for three days. On the first day Buddhists decorate their houses with lanterns, decorate their family shrine and light small bonfires. In Hiroshima, they put lights in little boats and float them down the river. In Kyoto, they light a huge fire on the hillside.

On the second day, there is a feast with music, games and a folk dance in which everyone takes part. There is also a stand decorated with lanterns. Monks visit as many homes as possible to recite scriptures in front of family shrines. This is to show respect for the visiting spirits of the families' ancestors.

On the third day, Buddhists make offerings of fruit and flowers at their family shrine. They ask for Buddha's blessing for their ancestors and say goodbye to the spirits.

Lanterns are lit before they are floated on a lake during O-bon celebrations.

The Buddhist calendar is a **lunisolar calendar**, which differs from the Western **Gregorian calendar**. Therefore, Buddhist holy days fall on different dates each year. Here are some of the major Buddhist festivals and celebrations:

Buddhist New Year

Mahayana Buddhists celebrate on the first full-moon day in January

Theravada Buddhists hold three-day celebrations from the first full moon in April

Magha Puja Day (Sangha Day)

Full-moon day of the third lunar month (March)

Wesak (Buddha Day)

First full-moon day in April or May

Asalha Puja Day (Dharma Day)

Full-moon day of the eighth lunar month (usually July)

O-bon or Ulambana (Ancestor Days)

From the first to the fifteenth day of the eighth lunar month (July or August)

Japanese Buddhists hold three-day celebrations in July or August

Loy Krathong (Festival of Floating Bowls)

Thai Buddhists celebrate on the full-moon night of the twelfth lunar month (usually November)

Important Buddhists

Two important Buddhists, famous for their good actions, are Cheng Yen, a Buddhist nun, and the fourteenth Dalai Lama.

Cheng Yen   1937–

Cheng Yen was born in 1937 in Taiwan and became a Buddhist nun. She originally planned to spend her life meditating. Then, one day, three Catholic nuns asked her why Buddhists did not build hospitals and schools like Christians do. Cheng Yen began fundraising by asking her fellow nuns to make baby shoes to be sold. They also made bamboo jars for people and asked them to put fifty cents in them each day for charity.

Cheng Yen founded a relief organization called the Buddhist Compassion Relief Tzu Chi Foundation. The Tzu Chi Foundation helps people in many countries, including Bangladesh, the Philippines, China, India, South America, and Ethiopia. Cheng Yen has also helped to establish a hospital, an elementary school, a kindergarten, a middle school, a college of technology, a nurse's college, a medical training center, a university, and a bone marrow data bank.

Cheng Yen

The Fourteenth Dalai Lama   1935–

The fourteenth Dalai Lama was born in 1935 in northeastern Tibet. He was named Llamo Dhondrub. When he was four he was recognized as the **reincarnation** of the thirteenth Dalai Lama. *Dalai Lama* means "teacher whose wisdom is as great as the ocean."

At the age of five, the Dalai Lama was enthroned as the spiritual leader of Tibet and began his monastic education. In 1950, aged only fifteen, he took on the political leadership of Tibet after China invaded in 1949. In 1959 the Dalai Lama was forced into **exile**. He was given protection by the Indian government and now lives in Dharamsala, in the foothills of the Himalayas.

The Dalai Lama has traveled all over the world campaigning for Tibet's independence. He also teaches and promotes values such as compassion, forgiveness, and religious harmony. In 1989, he was awarded the Nobel Peace Prize. If Tibet achieves independence, the Dalai Lama would like to return, not as a political leader but simply as a Buddhist monk.

From my own limited experience I have found that the greatest degree of inner tranquility comes from the development of love and compassion.

I do not believe that there has been an increase in the amount of people's hatred, only in their ability to manifest it in vastly destructive weapons.

THE FOURTEENTH DALAI LAMA

The fourteenth Dalai Lama

Clothes and Food

The choice of clothes for Buddhists depends on their country of birth and, most importantly, whether they are **lay people** or monks and nuns. Most Buddhists, whether lay or not, follow the precepts on food and mind-altering substances.

Clothes for Lay People

Buddhist lay people wear the clothes of their country. In Sri Lanka, for example, a Buddhist woman wears a sari. Sometimes when Buddhists celebrate special ceremonies they wear white.

Clothes for Monks and Nuns

This Buddhist nun wears white robes.

Buddhist monks and nuns wear saffron, maroon, yellow, or brown robes and have shaven heads and faces. They must give up all material things and this includes their hair and clothes. Sri Lankan Buddhist nuns wear white robes. Wearing the robes is a symbol of being willing to undertake the training.

Shoes

Everybody must take their shoes off before going into a temple, although shoes may be worn outside, around the temple area. Many monks do not wear shoes at all.

Shoes must be removed before entering a Buddhist temple.

กรุณาถอดรองเท้า

Buddhist monks eat food offered to them by Buddhist lay people.

Food and Drink

The First Precept says a Buddhist must avoid harming or taking the life of any living thing. For this reason many Buddhists are vegetarians. Buddhists are also expected to eat sensibly, which means not **fasting** too much and not eating too much. Buddha taught that it is important to follow the middle path, which means to avoid extremes.

Theravada monks and nuns usually do not eat after noon. They must eat to sustain their bodies but not because they are hungry.

Alcohol

The Fifth Precept tells Buddhists not to take anything that affects their thinking or makes them behave rashly, such as alcohol and drugs. If a person's mind is affected they cannot think clearly and they cannot meditate.

Birth

Babies born to Buddhist families have different rites of passage depending on the country in which the family lives.

Pregnancy and Labor in Tibet

When a Buddhist woman from Tibet becomes pregnant, she prays for a healthy child and an easy labor and visits the temple so that the monk or priest can bless her. She spends her pregnancy meditating and praying as much as she can so she becomes more relaxed and has an easier labor.

When she is in labor, her husband recites **mantras**. In the last stages of labor he feeds her butter that has been blessed.

After birth, butter may be put on the baby's tongue to symbolize good health, a long life, and always having enough to eat. Butter is then put on the tip of the baby's nose. The baby is cleaned with a cloth and warm water and wrapped tightly in cotton cloth and wool for warmth. The baby is then placed with the mother, who is given some hot butter, soup, and Tibetan tea to drink.

Meditation and prayer are very important throughout a Tibetan woman's pregnancy.

22

Baby Naming in Cambodia

When a baby is born to Buddhists in Cambodia, the family may ask a Buddhist monk to name the child. This is because the monk is wise and has had much life experience. The naming takes place three days to a week after the baby is born. It can be held at the same time as the baby shower, which is a party where the parents receive gifts for their baby.

The monk gives the baby's name lots of thought. He thinks about the date, the time of year, and the character of the child before he selects a name.

Parents may also choose the baby's name themselves. Some parents choose a name that helps them remember the day, month, or season when the baby was born. Others choose a name that rhymes with the mother's, father's, brother's, or sister's name. And some name their child after a flower, a star, the Sun, or the Moon.

A Buddhist baby-naming ceremony

Growing Up

Rites of passage for young Buddhists include attending dharma school and, for Theravada Buddhists, the Introduction to sangha.

Dharma School

Many Buddhist children and young people go to Saturday or Sunday school, which is also called dharma school. There they learn about Buddha's life and his teachings. These classes are held at Buddhist temples and the teachers include both parents and monks.

Themes that may be covered at dharma school include:

* faith
* Buddha's disciples
* practicing Buddhism
* **ethics**
* Buddhist traditions
* spirituality.

There is also a time of worship and a vegetarian meal, during or after dharma school.

Many young Buddhists attend dharma school.

Introduction to Sangha

In Theravada Buddhism, boys may participate in the Introduction to sangha. This allows them to be a novice monk for a short period, such as a day or a few months. This is often done when there is a death in the immediate family, such as a mother, father, grandmother, or grandfather. The **spiritual merits** gained from becoming a **novice monk** are dedicated to the family member who has passed on.

While participating in the Introduction to sangha, Theravada Buddhist boys lead the life of a monk. They must:

- have their head and eyebrows shaved
- learn the Ten Precepts for novice monks and nuns
- live at the monastery
- learn to meditate
- not wear shoes
- go on an **alms round**
- not eat after midday.

Young boys have their heads and eyebrows shaved when they become novice monks.

Marriage

A bride and groom being married in Vietnam wear colorful silk bhakus.

Buddhist wedding customs vary depending on the country in which a couple lives and the traditions they choose to follow. Different laws and customs also affect the roles of monks in the wedding ceremony.

Choosing a Partner

In Buddhist countries, parents often choose a wife or husband for their child. They believe parents are the most experienced as to what is right for their child. Horoscopes will be checked to make sure that the couple is well matched.

Wedding Clothes

A Buddhist bride may wear a type of dress called a bhaku and a sleeved blouse called a hanju. She may also wear a special coat and scarf, and jewelry around her neck, wrists, and forehead.

A Buddhist groom may wear a bhaku that reaches just above the ankles and has sleeves. He may also wear a waistcoat, a cap, and a sash.

Some Buddhists marry in Western style, with the bride wearing a white wedding dress and a veil and the groom wearing a suit and tie.

Wedding Ceremony

Traditional Buddhist weddings are often held at the family home or in a hotel. In recent times, though, weddings have also been held at Buddhist temples, conducted by Mahayana monks.

The bride and groom are led to a platform that has been decorated with white flowers. They promise to love and respect each other and then exchange rings. In Thailand and Sri Lanka, the thumbs on their right hands are tied together by the bride's uncle. Sometimes the couple's wrists are tied together with a silk scarf. This is a symbol that they are being joined together as husband and wife.

In Theravada Buddhism, monks are not allowed to conduct wedding ceremonies. The couple will first have a legal marriage ceremony and then visit a monastery. There they offer a **dana meal** to the sangha and their friends. A special blessing is chanted for the couple's future together and they may hear a sermon on Buddha's teachings about married life.

A Buddhist wedding ceremony in India

Death and the Afterlife

Buddhists see death as an inevitable part of their spiritual journey. They prefer the term "passing on" as they believe that they do not really die, but pass on to another realm.

Passing On

When Buddhists are dying, they like to have monks chanting blessings around them. This is to calm them and help them prepare to make the transition to rebirth.

Funerals

Mahayana Buddhists believe that there is an interval between passing on and rebirth. Therefore, it is strongly recommended that no one touch the body for three days.

Buddhists may be cremated or buried when they die, but are usually cremated. At the grave, monks recite the Three Jewels and the Five Precepts and read from Buddhist scriptures.

The Nan Tien Temple has an eight-story resting place.

Life After Death

Buddhists believe that after death, a person experiences bardo for forty-nine days. This is the state between passing on and rebirth into one of the six realms of the Wheel of Samsara. Only Buddhists who achieve enlightenment pass on to nirvana.

Rebirth

Buddhists believe that the actions performed in this life determine a person's karma and the realm in which they will be reborn. Someone who has been greedy and mean will go to pretas, where they will be hungry, thirsty, too hot, and too cold. Someone who spent all their time thinking about food, sleep, and sex will come back as an animal. Only when a person's karma is used up can they be reborn in a higher realm.

Nirvana

The aim of Buddhists is to become enlightened, like Buddha, so that they can escape being born over and over again. Nirvana is a state of perfect peace where there is no craving, no being disappointed, and, therefore, no suffering.

A depiction of the Buddha achieving enlightenment and ascending to nirvana.

Buddhism Around the World

Buddhism is the world's fourth-largest religion. There are approximately 360 million Buddhists around the world. Buddhists are mostly found in Asia, particularly Southeast Asian countries.

Theravada Buddhism is practiced in Sri Lanka, Myanmar (Burma), Thailand, Laos, and Cambodia, and parts of Malaysia, Vietnam, China, and Bangladesh. Mahayana Buddhism is practiced in China, Japan, Korea, and Vietnam.

Tibetan Buddhism is practiced in Tibet, Mongolia, Bhutan, and parts of Nepal, India, the Maldives, China, and Russia.

This map shows the top ten Buddhist countries.

ARCTIC OCEAN

ARCTIC OCEAN

MONGOLIA
50 percent

SOUTH KOREA
23 percent

BHUTAN
75 percent

PACIFIC OCEAN

ATLANTIC OCEAN

JAPAN
84 percent

MYANMAR (BURMA)
89 percent

LAOS
65 percent

SRI LANKA
69 percent

CAMBODIA
95 percent

PACIFIC OCEAN

THAILAND
95 percent

SINGAPORE
43 percent

INDIAN OCEAN

KEY

	area of country
CAMBODIA	name of country
95 percent	percentage of country population that is Buddhist

SOUTHERN OCEAN

SOUTHERN OCEAN

Glossary

abbot	leader of a monastery
alms round	daily round that many Theravada monks make, collecting gifts of food and other goods from lay people
bodhisattvas	enlightened people who have postponed nirvana to help other people achieve enlightenment
dalai lama	spiritual leader of Tibet
dana meal	meal which Buddhist lay people give to monks and nuns
deities	supernatural beings who provide rainfall, good crops, wealth, children, and protection
disciples	followers
ethics	a set of ideas as to the right way to act
exile	enforced absence from one's native country
fasting	not eating, or eating very little
Gregorian calendar	the most widely used calendar in the world, based on the cycle of the Sun
impermanent	does not last
incarnation	when a supernatural being is reborn in human form
karma	the belief that a person's actions in this life determine their destiny in the next life
lay people	Buddhists who are not monks or nuns
lunisolar calendar	a calendar based on the cycles of the Sun and the Moon
mantras	special verses said over and over again to help a person focus
nirvana	a state of great inner peace and contentment, when enlightenment has been achieved
novice monks	monks who have been received into a religious order but have not yet taken vows
pilgrimages	journeys, often long ones, made to sacred places or temples
prostrations	throwing yourself down in a sign of humility
realms	different worlds
reincarnation	to be reborn in another body or realm after death
scriptures	sacred writings
spiritual merits	spiritual credits granted for good actions
take refuge	to trust, rely on, and appreciate

Index